abond Poet Four Vagabond Poet Four Fo

Settle

Theresa Muñoz

Vagabond Voices
Glasgow

First published in March 2016 by
Vagabond Voices Publishing Ltd.,
Glasgow,
Scotland

ISBN 978-1-908251-63-3

Printed and bound in Poland

Cover design by Mark Mechan

Typeset by Park Productions

The publisher acknowledges subsidy towards
this publication from Creative Scotland

ALBA | CHRUTHACHAIL

For further information on Vagabond Voices, see the website,
www.vagabondvoices.co.uk

*For my father Arturo, whose
dream it first was*

Contents

Settle

Digital Life

Settle

Twenty-two

The age my mother and I emigrated to cities
we had never been, years apart

but some things were the same:
same church-like shuffle

down the jetway,
same keyhole window seeping light.

Same long-haul flight leaving us
sand-tongued, the chilled air

a punch in the face
when she landed mid-winter.

Surrounded by concrete towers,
she dropped her first payslip

down a gutter,
the snow landing like large moths.

And me from Vancouver to Glasgow,
35 Kelvinhaugh Gate, a flat so damp

I slept in a wool hat for months
and got lost coming back from a place

I'd been twice, so in a pub's doorway
I spread out my map, leaf-thin.

Once I heard her say,
twenty-two is the age I left Manila...

left the only patch of land she knew
to wonder as I did, on that cold step:

should I go back, or have I begun again?

Home

A piece of your childhood never confessed.
And I confess I heard it from him.
Those humid months
the family home was a broken-down bus.
Ditched beside a graffitied wall.
Two brothers and three sisters.
You the oldest.
Mostly I imagined the evenings.
Streetlight on the greasy windows.
Doors rattled by passing cars.
Each kid curled on a bench seat,
inhaling leather.
Grandpa, the driver, asleep at the wheel.
A bus poised for the road
but didn't go anywhere.

After Dad told me I watched you carefully,
for signs of old sadness.
A doctor, you took the train home from work,
if work lasted all night.
Glided down the escalator at seven am.
Fed a ticket into the blue machine.
Spied a window seat as the train pulled in.
It's how I imagined you coming home.
Blinking at the rails of sun in my room.
How to let you know I knew.
Could only blend you before and now:
asleep against the glass,
my mother's face lifted
by the day's long, long light.

Alma mater

Only the day I graduated
did he mention we share an alma mater.
My dad, a young man new to Canada.
His dark eyes filled
with trees and snow peaks,
as he strolled the wet concrete.

He was there, but fled to Toronto before Christmas.
Only one friend he mentioned:
that poet Earle Birney.
They wanted the same book in the library.
Birney smiled: *take it.*
Later Dad said: *He was ok, but I didn't like his poetry.*

In school I panicked on a question about Birney,
his poem 'Winter Saturday'.
Lines that went: *furred from the farmhouse,
like caterpillars from the wood.*
At seventeen I knew nothing of farmers,
had never glimpsed the Prairies.

Perhaps my dad was more puzzled than me.
That's why he decided to leave.
Slipped into dusk's pink glow after class.
No answers for why it rained
that day, yesterday and all of November.

And that was why he never said.
Until he drifted into the campus rose garden
above the ocean.
A hand dropped on my shoulder.
And I was astonished to hear
he had already seen the Pacific from that angle.

The way

In a new country, any kind of job will do.
My dad knew this

in the Toronto YMCA
eyeing the corkboard for work

for a day in the eraser factory
or sweeping the bank in his clip-on tie,

his pulse thudding
as he strode quickly

for the relief of plenty,
the sour smell of cash.

And I was new to Glasgow
working days in the uni gift shop,

selling t-shirts and magnets that read
Via veritas vita: the way the truth the life

so formal, like the clock
eyeing me when I came in on time

because my dad and I were never late,
never slept in.

And if a passerby in the rain could see
blue shirts hung in the corners

or the bank's white floor
flourishing a diamond gleam,

it was our way
back then, to measure our worth.

Simpsons department store, Toronto

My parents could have met in Manila
on a sweaty Jeepney
or down a market alley.
Instead, as two foreigners
not used to hats, scarves or heavy coats.

They laughed when I asked where.
Oh, in the stationary aisle.
Mom hunted a present for a nun,
Dad searched for paper clips.
Two years later, married at St. Michael's:
Dad in a rumpled suit, Mom in a bargain dress,
clutching winter roses.

But they could have met at a hospital.
The years uncovered this fact:
in Manila, Mom was nurse to Dad's sick aunt.
But back to the day in the stationary aisle.
Mom chose a fountain pen.
Dad said *That's a good present, for a nun.*

I tell their story to feel less lonely.
The sweet rush
of one leaving first, then the other
beyond the store's bold signs
and frosted steps,
into Toronto's starry expanse

as if this was how you came in,
came over,
twin dark heads in the snow.

Life in the UK

To take the test, I say aloud:
my name, my birthday, my hometown.

Desk clerk scans my navy passport.
You're from Canada?
My brother lives in Quebec, he loves to ski.
Why do you want to live here?'

To take the test, I step into a room.
Grey walls face the day's sun.
Computers hum their low song.
A Polish couple waits too.
They murmur: NHS, Ulster fry, Churchill.

I am alone. To take the test,
I studied for days. I know
all the English queens
the Glorious Revolution,
the cracked steps of the Giant's Causeway.

I know about haggis and home rule.
Who discovered the DNA molecule.
How to dispose of a broken fridge.
That it was the Iron Age
when coins were first shaped, or held.

Now the room fills like a boat.
To take this test, everyone pretends.
Beyond the room's fogged glass
and grid lights,
this will help us, help our new lives.

Desk clerk is kind but acts stern.
She gives us pink sheets to sign.
Screens flick on their grey gaze,
and I feel tense but ready in my arms.
She warns: *Once you press start
there's no turning back —*

Settlement

Leaves swirl above
old mattresses, chip wrappers
as we carry our documents:
rental agreements, bank statements
even the cat's adoption papers.

Inside we empty our pockets
surrender our phones, our coins
walk through the security gates
into a white room of booths
and crumpled magazines.

Hard not to peek
at the other applicants
leaning forward in their seats
clutching their numbered
tickets, gazing
at the overhead screens.

When it's our turn
I grip your fingers
as we show a stranger
our plans for the future
the jobs we have
the apartment we share:

here is our life,
on sheets
of paper.

Brand Street

By appointment they come,
a red-circled day on the calendar.

On the gum-splattered road they pause,
wondering how far down the building goes.

Some carry tea from the blue cafe nearby.
Most wear night-coloured clothes,

holding their dependents' sticky palms,
lugging a fat file

of money and paper, paper about money,
precious electric bills.

And when the guard says come in,
the whole day feels torn from them,

their mind's dull hum
replaced by crackling microphone sighs.

For hours it's the moon-textured walls.
White chairs melt into a white floor.

Ice

Some five thousand miles west
of our window, twelve players
skate around a white rink

and we huddle on the couch
at three, maybe four in the morning
with crisps and beer

crunching our way through
body-checks, fisticuffs,
penalty calls, goals flicked in

and when the camera pans
to Vancouver's night views
we lean forward to see

glass towers, mountain lights
cars streaming the Lions Gate bridge
to the silver stadium

where they loop the ice
and fling the puck
tiny and far   far

away.

Ashton Lane

We tell the story differently each time,
it's how we say it, we sound brave and braver.
Usually we start with the reek of sweat and metal,
how I saw him chatting up girls
and when those girls turned away

he slipped into our circle, sidled up to you
whispered something in your ear,
and you said: *who the hell are you?*
The man laughed with yellow teeth,
I said *what is this about* and —

it's funny, each time we get here, we laugh
about the slowest fight ever,
how the man reached for your neck with big thumbs,
you gripped both shoulders like a linebacker

toppling a ring of chairs, and voices echoed
hey! stop! hey! as you tumbled out
sliding on wet cobbles
into a zone of mud and cigarettes.

Then I kicked his ankle, kicked that gobstopper bone,
I was angry and ashamed
but I would do it again.
We left him choked as a fish
shouting about those immigrants

as we fell into a cab, slumped on tartan blankets
stroking the new welt under your eye
damning that phrase
the one we now say easily, jokingly, though it stings:
Hey— where did you buy her?

Skin

Nice tan said a man
leaning outside
The Captain's Rest.
Thanks I said
and kept on running,
already late meeting you
in Kelvingrove Park
where boys and girls sit
in half circles
on the clipped lawn
and old men wander
in dreamy lines
under the sun. Along
a line of seedlings
to a grove shaped
as a heart
I saw you watching
for me as one waits
for the beginning
of a song.
On a scratchy bench
we heard the fountain
drip and swirl
a two-beat humming
that made me wonder
what the man meant.
And whether
it was worth telling you,
in case my blush
was less the June heat
of a moist summer
but something
darker, redder, deeper.

Buchanan Street

Why do I stop at the top
looking down
at the cold blue lights
sloped stone walkway
and old rain glowing in the street?

Something to do with the change
in season, something about the early dark
and people strolling
flood-lit paths

takes me to that morning
at home, warm waking
in a red-roofed house
with rows of tulips

far from here, from the squeeze
of buses braking in turn
and police sirens sounding
in back lanes

and the hum of voices
in the crowd, whose
red and green shopping bags
nudge me

till I blink
breathe
continue down
Buchanan Street

Glasgow snowfall

wading through drifts
to reach the corner shop
snow
   (freezing my knees
sticking me
to the street)

   falling as I come across
another soul
on the sidewalk's edge

a short snow-drunk

with a pebble mouth
and stick arms, offering up
a fist-crushed can
of Tennent's lager –

the bright red T, stark
against the sudden whiteness
in breezy March, flakes
stinging my chin

and the can tipping
slightly
   to the wind

toasting me (slowly
covered in white): a

good morning

For me

Under grid lights at my local bank
a girl with coiled hair says:
Could you please sign this for me.
Could you type your pin for me.

Just a phrase, but the same phrase
at the shoe place, post office too.
For me... those words hold
a petal-like intimacy,
a light friendship
in this green country
where folk take their words
seriously, very seriously

so that an offhand phrase
said over foamy beers
with old, good friends
can split the air
of a tricky silence.

And it's these slim verbal lines,
speech's tripwires,
the sudden regretful pang
of a line I've said to hurt, or one that has hurt me
blurring my view
of the tiny coloured keys

so the girl with the coiled hair
must say again, in her gentle voice
making me wonder if we could be friends
please enter your pin,
for her, for me.

Travelling

holding your gaze

salt and wet cotton –
the smell
of leaving

*

at security
I shrug off my jacket
pull off my shoes
pad through the frame

avoiding the face
of the woman whose hands
slide down my sides

*

am I, or am I not
falling out of the sky

the low rumbling
the bouncing

in my seat I feel it coming,
its unkind wave chasing

the future

*

where were we
when we said goodbye?

your hand on my back
our smiles stretched
the din of others around us
minutes sliding past

*

nothing so difficult
as getting further
further away

the landscape
from the window slows
hard ice to ocean

*

daylight wakes me
some place new

light spills
over me, into the aisles

leaving you
on my mind
leaving you

as we descend
into overwhelming brightness

Come home

and everyone so kind, seeing you now
        for who you have
            become

careful, deliberate; in the doorway
        their eyes show
            a new opinion

light falls along the stairs
        to the bed
            you sleep well in

in the darkness of the room
        your mind wanders
            into oblivion

in the centre
        of the low bed
            you're small again

You in winter

That day our car veered
into a ditch

and you stepped out
hatless, backwards

onto the frozen grass
by the snow-streaked road

to gaze
at the speckled sky

black capillaries of winter trees

or to count, in your bemused way
the swinging falling flakes

touching the upturned collar
of your blue coat

On a lake

in an old canoe, knowing
it's true: I like

being here, under the blurred
bodies of pines

and the curved gloomy edges
of fog, not feeling lonely

or declarative just hoping
and paddling slowly

pushing the dark blue water
behind me

in this wet overturn
of September into autumn, how

the leaves come down
to be with the lilies

the frogs sing out
squatting on a log

Close

huddled, cold
in a cave

of smooth tenement
brick

watching

brief wet textures fall
diagonally

like lines

drawn solid
across paper

a way

of cross-hatching
the air

On Arthur's Seat

How do I lean into nothing

walk to the cliff edge
and look over without

falling, like on train platforms
how black those ground wires

and how near to the yellow line
should people loiter

what's the rule now
for getting close to danger,

things in tight passing — cars, buses,
strangers — how safe are we

in rooms of early light
with others we get to know slowly

and how much of our pasts
is too hard to explain

or too tricky, what would happen
if I strode along stamped grass

peered over the edge
into emptiness

trusting myself to the town's tiny lights.

Dart

Coming to see you

I became a dart, flung
down the river path

my needle head, my barrel-grips
and my spiked tail so crucial

to my flying arc,
and I thought only of becoming light

in my curve, of racing weightless
over hedge rows

and pink-flowered trees,
and when I hit my target

of my wind-swept flight,
I'd declare myself new.

I was ready,
but I was thrown badly

from my hilly side of town
to your flat by the chilled bay

and the weight of old thoughts bore down
in an echoed thud

when I knocked too hard, all fists, at your door.

East Preston Street Cemetery

born August
sons
two summers ago

third in the seventh row
bold typeset

from time to time
curled poinsettia
red card inside

yesterday before lunch
of a woman's red coat

whose footsteps
then loop round
following

he had a family
died at sixty

speckled black granite
sprinkling of snow

gifts come and go
foil-wrapped box
an ivory envelope

spotting the collar
I pulled back the curtain to see

pause at his grave
the broken trees
my own

Zoo

We agree to reconvene in a few hours
because you would like the Picasso,
and I want the animals.

Alone, the afternoon stretches out.
I pay seventeen euros
damp from my pockets

and wander
with a broken sandal
around the drowsy creatures

yawning hippos
bowed flamingos
and jungle cats curled

in their wire enclosures.
Only the monkeys
swipe and holler.

All I want is to find you.
Sweaty and blistered
with a crumpled zoo flyer

I edge the perimeters
and see you standing
beyond the exit's turnstiles

and we are freed,
the instant we catch sight
of each other.

Vows

This is the only type of love I can promise.

The type that duct tapes out the winter draught
or waits till after midnight on the couch,
to not disrupt your night out.

Or goes to the supermarket
in the slanting rain
for twice-forgotten milk.

And saves you the best of everything:
window seat, the bigger half, the last bite.

The kind pledging to be
your best friend, co-editor and wife.

And wants nothing more than to
read your words, style your hair,
fill your plate each night

promising to see the world together,
linger at the corner table together,
until our last day's light.

Referendum day

For days I tried to name a sign,
a sign foretelling the end.
Maybe the city wind,
or the coastal fog that stayed.

Your dark blue tie and my dress the same shade.
The window debates:
YES spelled out with packing tape,
and the cross in the O of No Thanks
winking mean like a pirate's face.

It was our stroll by the Parliament that night,
thick with teens draped in flags.
A fiddler perched on the fountain rim,
and when phones began to film
a glow spread,
spread into the water-light.

A sign, I realised, that couldn't be seen.
The messages from
the broadcasting tent
beside the Parliament,
filtering into our homes.

So small, we missed it the first time round.
The pennies in the fountain we passed.
Tiny coins holding our hopes.

Digital Life

Trail

could there be a way to see you always

not just in the rooms we enter
linger   breathe in silent sync

but as a way of tracking your location:

your feet along Princes St
past blocks of art galleries
stamping up the Playfair steps

or in the basement of the library
hunched over broken desks

maybe we could deploy that shirt,
the one I bought you
a city map on burgundy cloth

I'd slip it on while you were out:
you'd be the red dot running

down my olive shoulders

nestling into my wrist

my rushing pulse

Author photo

Her job is to archive items in a university library.
One day, a dusty box of author photos.
She lays out a chessboard of faces.
Some writers look frail, already elderly.
Or like boxers, hunched and solitary.
They are foragers, close to trees.
Hypnotists, with a serious gaze.
Like academics, paid to be wise.
Autumn goes on forever: everyone wears sweaters.
Dressed in black, like mourners.
Guilty, as if these are mugshots.
Only their wild hair, smoothed over the years
gives each particular heart away.

I zoom your face

My cursor stirs   the blurred pink pixels
of your low-resolution photo

I play with your swirling face
slim nose   penny-brown eyes
rippled slope of your throat

I can make you stamp-size
your face from twenty yards
drifting to me   my spot on the street

or actual size   your face fleshy as mine
two heads on thick carpet
reading the same book

there's miles between us
but distance is conquerable
you could return

if I keep sweeping
your dark brow
chin bottom lip

your face zoomed in
as if right here
talking back, in whispers

Be the first to like this

kicking pine cones down the street
climbing the backyard cherry tree
lying in new sheets
waking in darkness   waking to snow
how your chest thickens when you're scared
how my voice bubbles when you're pleased
be the first to like
view of wind turbines from the train
golden tint on a glass of wine
gliding on rollerblades by the sea
waking so warm   waking on the beach
how your eyes flood when you're tired
how you laugh when you're relieved
like bridges creeks frisbees
silly cat videos and Instagram photos
like strolling with a friend
between folds of trees
and your heart rolls out a big pink wave
and your lips recall something sweet
like skiing and ice-skating
zip-lining above trees at seventy clicks
like every new experience because it was new
to me   pocketed in your memory
like the first time I fed the ducks
at Stanley Park
and they stormed like villagers
to my feet

How

how to get up in the dark
how to get out of debt

how to find your keys
how to find the courage

how to run a business
how to run long distances

how to build confidence
how to build credit

how to be a better listener
how to be a better lover

how to relax
how to rewrite

how to live on little money
how to live without anybody

how to stop losing
when to stop googling

Phone

His is a rumbling brick,
a metal heart
buzzing his chest
from within his pocket.

Mine, a tiny satellite
or treasure box
collecting envelope icons,
numbers, voicemail pings.

One night I did this over and over.
Scrolling down
I punched a key
and like a wish granted
your voice (without you knowing)
bellowed

Hi you've reached —
Hi, you've reached —

Delete where appropriate

if only we   had a record
of everything we ever said
a silver typewriter
that clicked and published
our words and sighs   as they evaporated
if only we had a transcript
of our bad years   our better ones
a list of criticisms spat
across the kitchen
a register of kind phrases
uttered before bed   or in the car
my hand on your thigh
in the melting dark   if only we

had a database   a spreadsheet
we could search the terms
of our agreement
had we bothered   to write one
had we been honest
about ourselves   our wishes and failings
perhaps I wouldn't be
on the bottom stair
eyes pressed into my knees
conjuring looping screeds   of ivory paper
that I could amend   delete where appropriate

Friends

share your existence with friends
share the best days of your life

connect with people worldwide
connect by your lamp's single light

find faces you once kissed in the dark
find those you left behind

read their rage on war, politics, oil
know nothing of their real sorrow

scroll their stream-of-consciousness posts
read an edited voice

'like' wedding snaps and graduation caps
mourn your tiny achievements

frown when you find one friend gone
lie awake, wonder what you've done

unfriend a childhood pal, a workmate,
your sibling in one click

say nothing of it

Filed under 'unfinished'

sandwich crumbs

swig of beer in the glass

rugby scarf, half-knitted

soap carving of a rabbit

(things of small value, but with her imprint)

PhD in linguistics

Chopin piano nocturnes

Spanish

half marathon

essay on lichen

(things, for varied reasons, abandoned)

February romance

beach walk at high tide

second driving test

chat with her dad near his beside

(the hardest things; things finished for her)

Google page twenty

Poor google page twenty adrift in the internet desert
nobody comes to click on you witness your existence barely I
in my sixth hour of searching for pear trees in the backwoods
of British Columbia you are the product of random words
pear trees / grow / Canada and the frustrated insistence of return, return
every topic and / or search terms in the world has a Google page twenty
the straight-backed Ariel font, the friendly open letters and
delicate coded strings greater than / less than percentages
and the ever so polite *Is this what you mean?* to search for the net of gathering
stories from all around the world about the man who grew pear trees
to save his family from drowning and a picture of a cat who climbs pear trees
and me in the back room study bleary-eyed at 3am but unable to
stop clicking, clicking where outside the trees
are filled with unrest and I am clicking alone but not as lonely are you.

All the words she whispers before sleep

100, 99, 98
cold coffee
grey stones
salty grass
tire track
toughen up
ten weeks left
97, 96, 95, 94
square branch
wood flake
ariel fonts
part truths
orange moon
92, 91, 90, 89
koi pond
blue lights
the restaurant
wish I hadn't
wish I hadn't now
88, 87,86
oceans
the shape of him
dark swim
eyes make wet clicks
85, 84, 83, 83.

All the places

were you there   did you see
the unfinished glory of the Sagrada Família

did you take a train across Europe   across Canada
did your brain burst from boredom along the Prairies

could we have been in the same place   at the same time
twin gondolas under the Bridge of Sighs

or have you been   all the places I have
just without me years before

the bowed trace of your lips   on small white coffee cups
the tread of your boots on Scottish beaches

are you here now   on this dripping April night
not quite asleep not quite wanting to

your eyes two triangles   your hair an arched wave
your shirt a bed of rivers crinkling towards your face

Digital life

I found a way to keep you around:

if I type your name
into the search engine
your crisp gaze beams
from each small box

and if I click below those images
it's your moniker
on this book review beside three black stars

consider how your voice appears
in your last funny tweet
about bananas, of all things

and if I read LinkedIn employment
I count the solid straight years
you lost, or gave

as the screen glows and sighs
and the streetlights click on
I stream your video channel,

starting with the slim man
singing on the beach
in the crushed dark

coming closer,
his face filling the screen
where nothing really lives, I know.

Junk

Dear most trusted friend,
spirits led me to you.
Your relative of the same name has died.
You are the beneficiary of a heavenly sum.
Give me the number of your safe foreign account.
I know I can trust you,
an outsider like me.
I will come to your country,
cross oceans of pink squid
and the dreaming whale.
We will divide fairly: forty-sixty
and find ways to spend the money.
I wait urgently for your reply!
Your loving friend,
your loving friend far away,
(there is no catch I promise).

Googling the Other Theresas

If I could be one of them,
I'd paint in watercolours, deserts with low suns
in my life's last month

or I'd be an athlete, chasing the cork path
my chin level
till I crossed, sweat lacing my neck

or I'd be a surgeon in blue scrubs
mending others with precise cuts
and their grateful eyes after

would be enough, or high on heroin
I'd rob a corner store
and plunge a steak knife

into a man's apple heart,
and before my damning mugshot
before the camera clicked twice,

it would all become real.
And I could become real.

When laptops die

they go.

Like ours, their bodies pack up and die.
A film clogs their webcam eye.
Their battery hearts slow.

And when they go, so too our pasts.
Our documents:
cover letters, budget reports
beach selfie under azure sky.

If laptops have a heaven,
it is an air-conditioned room.
Or the store they were bought,
wrapped in clingfilm.

Witness
to our sexual trysts,
our critical sweeping gaze,
our naked skin,
our impromptu jigs when pleased.
For this we owe them big.

So when they release
their last fan-churned breath
how else to mourn
but tenderly wipe their screen face,
ceremonially close their lids.

Holiday selfie

She goes on holiday with her sister
to Copenhagen, a city of looping canals.
They are a part of the landscape,
but do not own it.
In them are fillable spaces,
small secret worlds,
a wish to lay claim.
The camera above her head
like a tiny sun,
snapping her chin
by the old wharf,
the sea's passionate surface.
On holiday their bodies
slow down, they drift
from stately opera house
to wood and brick castle,
cast themselves
in their grand watery shadow.

A button, a flash, a means
to bind ourselves
to a new land –
maybe, maybe not.
Still they seek a new home.
In the crunch of new snow
they pose beside the art gallery,
snap and pause,
decide if they belong,
walk crookedly on.

Wait

There is not one word to describe how it feels.
Only scenes reflecting an inner state.
On my walk home, low mist enfolds North Bridge.
Green bins collect emptiness.
Streetlights don't blink but wince.
Rain slides down the alley bricks.
Coming in and fixing a drink,
I recall a childhood beach
when I lifted a shell and held it to my ear
as the shapes and colours of my family
grew less and less
and I had to run, run to catch up with them.

No emails from you when I check.

Clicksend

And when she's too sad to talk   her fingers tap and text
grocery items in emoji spaghetti apple vodka pear
clicksend a hug, a hug across oceans   to her sister in Canada
pink flower petal face   *clicksend* her date hasn't arrived
frustration at being left she gives the thumb-edge
Are you on your way? ? clicksend

texting suits a quiet time   a little voice
to her only work-friend *Would you like one?*
one coffee with a steam-tail
some days it's her own voice   spinning around the world
I'm nobody, nobody and comes back   *clicksend*

Her favourite email

lives in her phone.
She reads it on the bus as the sky slips blue to black.

The email is from a friend across the ocean.
Dear Theresa. How is the PhD?
In what magazine is your poem?
How are you getting on?

And then: *You are nearly there,*
sending love your way.
Those words like a hand,
a hand cupping her face,
to smooth over a bad day

and the email's full stops
become the street's unlit lights,
the moist dots of her eyes.

Refresh

Each furious click
in the slow spell of night
means there's a missing
part to her life, beyond
these tiny words lost
in empty white

Coming to Scotland

I come from a family of immigrants, though I never thought of us that way until I became an immigrant myself. My father's ancestors migrated to the Philippines from Madrid, taking the name Muñoz with them. My mother's grandfather was from Taiwan. As legend goes, the family name was Tan but after arrival, my great-great grandfather changed the surname to Tansingco. The second part was derived from the Spanish word "cinco", indicating that five Tans had made the journey. The change of name also had the effect of making it sound more Filipino and thus tapping in to the most basic desire of most immigrants – the desire to fit in.

My parents immigrated to Canada separately from the Philippines in 1970. They met in the stationery aisle at Simpson's department store in Toronto. I imagine them now as they were then: two small, young, dark-haired people who had never seen snow before they flew north. I wrote about them in a poem entitled "Simpsons department store, Toronto":

They laughed when I asked where.
Oh, in the stationary aisle.
Mom hunted a present for a nun,
Dad searched for paper clips.
Two years later, married at St. Michael's:
Dad in a rumpled suit, Mom in a bargain dress,
clutching winter roses.
But they could have met at a hospital.
The years uncovered this fact:
in Manila, Mom was nurse to Dad's sick aunt.

But back to the day in the stationary aisle.
Mom chose a fountain pen.
Dad said *That's a good present, for a nun.*

Several years later, it was my turn to continue the family tradition when I moved to Scotland to do a Masters in Creative Writing at Glasgow University with poet Tom Leonard as my tutor. I had never been to Glasgow before. My parents sewed £700 in cash into a secret pocket inside my jeans, perhaps imagining the worst. I ended up working two days a week at the Glasgow University gift shop, where I explored a connection with my father in a poem called "The way":

> In a new country, any kind of job will do.
> My dad knew this
> in the Toronto YMCA
> eyeing the corkboard for work
> for a day in the eraser factory
> or sweeping the bank in his clip-on tie,
> his pulse thudding
> as he strode quickly
> for the relief of plenty,
> the sour smell of cash.

My course at Glasgow University was challenging, sociable, and over too quickly in one year. When it ended, I decided to make Scotland my home. I applied for and received the now-defunct Fresh Talent visa that lasted for two years. I worked as an events planner for a new-age classical ensemble at the Centre for Contemporary Arts and freelanced for the *Herald* and *The List*. I then received a student visa and an Overseas Research Student scholarship to do a PhD in Scottish Literature on the work of Tom Leonard. In the meantime, I published a poetry pamphlet called *Close* and moved to Edinburgh where I work as a researcher and tutor.

Several years and many wallet-crippling visas later, my partner and I found ourselves nervously waiting outside an Edinburgh New Town office. I was there to sit the "Life in the United Kingdom" test which is a required part of the permanent settlement process. My partner took my well-thumbed copy of the official preparatory guide and waited for me in a cafe across the road. I opened the navy blue door feeling slightly bereft without my book which I had been studying for weeks.

I found the book heavy on English history as I set out to learn it verbatim. Though there are focus questions at the end, it was difficult to discern what is important and what is not. The test may be "purely trivial", as one professor of public policy described it, but that is no comfort to those who actually have to pass it. As much as anything, it seems to be assessing the applicant's language level, which is another contentious issue in today's immigration debates.

The test was mandatory if I wanted to stay in the UK. I was disappointed that there is little evidence of Scottish life beyond Edinburgh. The few Scottish topics seeded through the index included: Edinburgh Castle, Bannockburn, Chris Hoy, Andy Murray and haggis. Our wonderful Scottish Parliament gets only a brief mention. I think I also found a mistake: the book contends that £50 is the highest currency denomination in the UK but Scottish and Northern Ireland banks issue £100 notes.

I wrote about the process in my poem "Life in the UK":

> I am alone. To take the test,
> I studied for days. I know
> all the English queens
> the Glorious Revolution,
> the cracked steps of the Giant's Causeway.
> I know about haggis and home rule.
> Who invented the DNA molecule.
> How to dispose of a broken fridge.
> That it was the Iron Age
> when coins were first shaped, or held.

Back in the New Town, the test was administered by two kindly women who took time to register each test-taker beforehand. Upon seeing my passport, one told me cheerfully that her brother lived in Montreal and he loved to ski. She seemed surprised that I was so keen to live in Scotland. I sat with other applicants in a grey airless room staring at the thin-necked computer screens. Pencils and lined paper were doled out. We were told there were no second chances: 'Once you press start, there's no turning back'.

I felt the way I used to before childhood races, when you stood tense before the line. I pressed start eagerly. Multiple-choice question emerged on the screen. As I clicked through the test, I was surprised to find that only 3 of 24 were directly related to Scotland. What is the maximum amount that can be dealt with in Scottish small claims court? What is the function of the Sherriff Court in Scotland? Where did Bonnie Prince Charlie raise his army? In addition, the universities of Glasgow and Edinburgh provided a comedy option in a question about which British universities competed in the boat race. I was disappointed not to be asked one of the questions I had giggled at during a previous practice test: "The Westminster Government consists of the House of Commons, House of Lords, House of Fraser (pick two from three)."

Everyone was given 45 minutes, though I admit I finished in a lightning-quick seven. I alerted the administrators and was herded into a side waiting room, eventually followed by some of the other applicants. We sat drinking water from the cooler and tried to smile at each other, though the atmosphere was tense. Eventually I was called to the desk. A young woman said "Congratulations – you passed." "What score did I get?" I asked her, ever curious. She said that they didn't give out that information; they only let you know if you passed or failed. "So you can tell everyone you got a perfect score!" she continued. Leaving the centre, I saw people with disappointed faces; they were not so lucky and would have to take the test again.

As I walked excitedly down the street to be reunited with my partner, I speculated about questions I may have got wrong. I was tripped up by one about the Home Secretary's responsibilities. I didn't include policing as I was confused by the fact that it is on the Justice Secretary's patch in Scotland.

In truth, the process of settlement wasn't quite over.

The pass certificate was just another piece of paper that had to be added to the pile that I had been collecting for years. It already included gas bills, evidence of tax returns, pay slips, job contracts, rental agreements, doctor's letters, photographs, and so on. There were long forms to fill in and many pages of identity, solvency, residence and occupational proof had to be photocopied. A week later I presented myself and my life well-documented to the United Kingdom Border Agency in Brand Street in Glasgow. Four hours later, I battled my way through the Govan wind and rain as a "New Scot". The system that took me in as an international student years ago had finally permitted me to become a permanent resident, and I'm happy that it did.

The question I am asked most frequently these days is: "Why did you leave Canada for Scotland?" It's a good question and one that I find difficult to answer. Canada is a multicultural country with low-cost healthcare, a very high standard of healthy living and excellent universities. I was born and raised on the West Coast with its rugged mountain ranges, orca-filled sea and warm summers. But while at university, I sensed a growing materialism and a desire to always have the best of everything: food, wine, holiday and house. And sometimes living in a city of such stagey, towering beauty can feel oppressive, or numbing. You can grow afraid to not be happy all the time.

I was 22 when I packed two suitcases (one of clothes, the other of books) to come to Glasgow. I have lived in Scotland for several years now and see so many things to love about it. It's liberating to be around so many people who take politics, culture, history and literature so seriously. There is an imperative in Scotland to be bold, honest, critical and not to be afraid to speak your mind. It's true that people can speak gruffly or sharply which unnerved me at first, until I understood the inherent kindness in the voices. I see a lot of compassion for others here and people committed to making the place better. People take friendships very seriously and that is something I have grown to appreciate and depend upon.

Being a poet in Scotland has also been a positive and encouraging experience. Here I have reviewed books by Scottish authors, interviewed writers, and published poems in several journals. My recent inclusion in the Scottish Poetry Library's *Best Scottish Poems* and appearances at Scottish literature festivals make me feel part of the current scene. These are things I never thought I would get the chance to do. The longer I stay, the more I feel myself drawn deeper into Scotland.

Even so, being a visible minority, I stand out in Scotland in a way that I never did in Canada. One afternoon while I was running to meet friends in Kelvingrove Park, a man leaning in the doorway of a pub yelled "Nice tan" at me. Other people around him laughed. Once when I was reading in a Glasgow coffee shop, three local kids plunked themselves across from me couch. I smiled at them and in response they pulled at the corners of their eyes, asking: "Are you Chinese?" I am often surprised to be asked where I am *really* from when I answer Canada. I am tired of having to insist that I am not Chinese (or a "Chinky" as one taxi driver put it seemingly without intending to offend). Once, an elderly man in the public library in Dumfries asked me if I was from the Far East and I said "Yes, I'm from Edinburgh." These things happen less often now than they used to and I wonder if I am presenting myself differently. Not so diffident perhaps, but pleased to be here, settled here, belonging here.

Still, the public narrative in Britain concerning immigration isn't very helpful. Canada is a country of immigrants and it would be electoral suicide for even a right-wing government to suggest that immigration and multiculturalism aren't good things. Here, the loudest voices often say the opposite. This can still occasionally get personal. I delivered a speech to a National Collective gathering in which I said some positive things about multiculturalism. When the text was posted to the NC website, someone commented that they wanted no part of this in Scotland ("the country of my birth"). The anonymous person also told me that if I supported a multicultural society, I should go live in London or, bizarrely, Pakistan. Later, I attended a panel session on immigration at the Festival of Politics at the Scottish Parliament and a handful of loudmouthed, ruddy-faced, rather scary men in the audience made it quite clear what they thought about immigrants.

I take comfort, however, in the bigger picture. At the same panel at the Festival of Politics, the vocally anti-immigrant men were opposed by almost everyone else in the room. I have heard MSPs of various political stripes speak out in favour of immigration, while I've read pro-immigration editorials in Scottish newspapers. The immigration reforms that enabled my parents to move to Canada in the first place weren't just about immigration. They allowed Canada to shed its edge-of-empire legacy and become bigger in a metaphorical sense and better in every sense. This is something Scotland can do too if it chooses and more people can have the wonderful experiences I've had.

Acknowledgements

Some of the following poems appeared in these journals: *Best Scottish Poems 2013, Canadian Literature, Causeway / Cahbsair, Echolocation, The Frogmore Papers, Gutter, New Linear Perspectives, New Leaf, Northwords Now, New Writing Scotland 26, 28, 29, 30, Poetry Review, Poetry Scotland, Stand, The Red Wheelbarrow, Under the Radar,* and *Valve.*

Some poems also appeared in *Close* (HappenStance Press, 2012). "All the places I have" was a prize-winner in the McLellan Poetry Prize, 2012. "Simpson's Dept Store, Toronto" was a prize-winner in the Troubadour International Poetry Prize, 2013. "I zoom your face" was exhibited at The Written Image, Edinburgh Printmakers 2013. "Be the first to like this" is the title poem of a volume of Scottish poetry from Vagabond Voices, 2014. "Author's Photo" was written as a response to the "Poetics of the Archive: Bloodaxe Books" project run by the Newcastle Centre for the Literary Arts. A draft of this collection was shortlisted for the Melita Hume Poetry Prize 2014.

"Coming to Scotland" was first published as "Becoming A Scot" in the *Scottish Review of Books*, Volume 10, Issue 2, Spring 2014.

I'm indebted to Colin Waters for his editing and constant reassurance, and to Allan Cameron and the Vagabond Voices team for taking on the book. Thank you to Iain Clark for his wonderful author photographs and to James Robertson and Tom Leonard for their encouragement. Heartfelt appreciation goes to my parents Arturo and Helen, my sisters Dulce, Stella and Lori and their families, and to Puma. For their unfailing good humour and friendship, I'm grateful to Mary Paulson-Ellis, Pippa Goldschmidt, Allan Radcliffe, George Anderson, Andrew Roberts and Isabelle McGrath. Much love to Pamela Dalziel, Helena Nelson and Susan Muir for their kindness over the years. And to Harry, whose love has meant everything.